TO MOTHERS

CARRYING THE TORCH OF FAITH AND FAMILY

JEFFREY R. HOLLAND
PATRICIA T. HOLLAND

DESERET
BOOK

Salt Lake City, Utah

Art direction by Richard Erickson
Cover and interior design by Sheryl Dickert Smith
Cover and interior images © Shutterstock/Curly Pat/Irtsya
Book design © 2016 Deseret Book Company

© 2016 Jeffrey R. Holland and Patricia T. Holland

Library of Congress Cataloging-in-Publication Data

(CIP data on file)
ISBN 978-1-62972-211-5

Printed in the United States of America
Publishers Printing, Salt Lake City, UT

10   9   8   7   6   5   4   3   2

Contents

Behold Thy Mother

JEFFREY R. HOLLAND

Prophesying of the Savior's Atonement, Isaiah wrote, "He hath borne our griefs, and carried our sorrows" (Isaiah 53:4). A majestic latter-day vision emphasized that "[Jesus] came into the world . . . to bear the sins of the world" (D&C 76:41). Both ancient and modern scripture testify that "He redeemed them, and bore them, and carried them all the days of old" (see Isaiah 63:9; D&C 133:53). A favorite hymn pleads with us to "Hear your great Deliv'rer's voice!" ("Israel, Israel, God Is Calling," *Hymns* [1985], no. 7).

Bear, borne, carry, deliver. These are powerful,

heartening messianic words. They convey help and hope for safe movement from where we are to where we need to be—but cannot get without assistance. These words also connote burden, struggle, and fatigue; words most appropriate in describing the mission of Him who, at unspeakable cost, lifts us up when we have fallen, carries us forward when strength is gone, delivers us safely home when safety seems far beyond our reach. "My Father sent me," He said, "that I might be lifted up upon the cross; . . . that as I have been lifted up . . . even so should men be lifted up . . . to . . . me" (3 Nephi 27:14).

But can you detect in this language another arena of human endeavor in which we use words like *bear* and *borne, carry* and *lift, labor* and *deliver*? As Jesus said to John while in the very act of Atonement, so He says to us all, "Behold thy mother!" (John 19:27).

I echo sentiments that have been expressed before when I say that no love in mortality comes closer to approximating the pure love of Jesus

Christ than the selfless love a devoted mother has for her child. When Isaiah, speaking messianically, wanted to convey Jehovah's love, he invoked the image of a mother's devotion. "Can a woman forget her sucking child?" he asks. How absurd, he implies, though not as absurd as thinking Christ will ever forget us (Isaiah 49:15).

This kind of resolute love "suffereth long, and is kind . . . seeketh not her own . . . but . . . beareth all things, believeth all things, hopeth all things, endureth all things" (Moroni 7:45; 1 Corinthians 13:4–7). Most encouraging of all, such fidelity "never faileth" (Moroni 7:46; 1 Corinthians 13:8). "For the mountains shall depart and the hills be removed," Jehovah said, "but my kindness shall not depart from thee" (3 Nephi 22:10; see also Isaiah 54:10). So, too, say our mothers.

You see, it is not only that they bear us but they continue bearing *with us*. It is not only the prenatal carrying but the lifelong carrying that makes mothering such a staggering feat. Of course there are heartbreaking exceptions, but most mothers know intuitively, instinctively that this is a sacred trust of the highest order. The weight of that realization, especially on young maternal shoulders, can be very daunting.

A wonderful young mother recently wrote to me, "How is it that a human being can love a child so deeply that you willingly give up a major portion of your freedom for it? How can mortal love be so strong that you voluntarily subject yourself to responsibility, vulnerability, anxiety, and heartache and just keep coming back for more of the same? What kind of mortal love can make you feel, once you have a child, that your life is never, ever your own again? Maternal love *has* to be divine. There is no other explanation for it. What mothers do is an essential element of Christ's work. Knowing that should be enough to tell us the impact of such love will range between unbearable and transcendent, over and over again, until with the safety and salvation of the very last child on earth, we can [then] say with Jesus, '[Father!] I have finished the work which thou gavest me to do'" (John 17:4).

With the elegance of that letter echoing in our minds, let me share three experiences reflecting the majestic influence of mothers:

My first account is a cautionary one, reminding us that not every maternal effort has a storybook ending, at least not immediately. That reminder stems from my conversation with a beloved friend of more than fifty years who was dying outside the faith and away from this Church he knew in his heart to be true. No matter how much I tried to comfort him, I could not seem to bring him peace. Finally he leveled with me. "Jeff," he said, "however painful it is going to be for me to stand before God, I cannot bear the thought of standing before my mother. The gospel and her children meant everything to her. I know I have broken her heart, and that is breaking mine."

Now, I am absolutely certain that upon his passing his mother received my friend with open, loving arms; that is what parents do. But the cautionary portion of this story is that children *can* break their mothers' hearts. Here, too, we see another comparison with the divine. I need not remind us that Jesus died of a broken heart, one weary and worn out from bearing the sins of the world. So, in any moment of temptation, may we "behold [our] mother" as well as our Savior and spare them both the sorrow of our sinning.

Second, I speak of a young man who entered the mission field worthily, but by his own choice returned home early due to same-sex attraction and some trauma he experienced in that regard. He was still worthy, but his faith was at crisis level, his emotional burden grew ever heavier, and his spiritual pain was more and more profound. He was by turns hurt, confused, angry, and desolate.

His mission president, his stake president, his bishop spent countless hours searching and weeping and blessing him as they held on to him, but much of his wound was so personal that he kept at least parts of it beyond their reach. The beloved father in this story poured his entire soul into helping this child, but his very demanding employment circumstance meant that often the long, dark nights of the soul were faced by just this boy and his mother. Day and night, first for weeks, then for months that turned into years, they sought healing together. Through periods of bitterness (mostly his but sometimes hers) and unending fear (mostly hers but sometimes his), she bore—there's that beautiful, burden-some word again—to her son her testimony of God's power, of His gospel, of His Church, but especially of His love for this child. In the same breath she testified of her own uncompromised, undying love for him as well. To bring together those two absolutely crucial, essential pillars of her very existence—the gospel of Jesus Christ and her family—she poured out her soul in prayer endlessly. She fasted and wept, she wept and fasted, then she listened and listened as this son repeatedly told her of how his heart was breaking. Thus she carried him—again—only this time it was not for nine months. This time she thought that laboring through the battered landscape of his despair would take forever.

But with the grace of God, her own tenacity, and the help of scores of Church leaders, friends, family members, and professionals, this importuning mother has seen her son come home to the promised land. Sadly we acknowledge that such a blessing does not, or at least has not yet, come to all parents who anguish over a wide variety of their children's circumstances, but here there was hope. And, I must say, this son's sexual orientation did not somehow miraculously change—no one assumed it would. But little by little his heart changed.

He started back to church. He chose to partake of the sacrament willingly and worthily. He again obtained a temple recommend and accepted a call to serve as an early-morning seminary teacher, where he was wonderfully successful. And now, after *five years* he has, at his own request and with the Church's assistance, reentered the mission field to complete his service to the Lord. I have wept over the courage, integrity, and determination of this young man and his family to work things out and to help him keep his faith. He knows he owes much to many, but he knows he owes the most to two messianic figures in his life, two who bore him and carried him, labored with him and delivered him—his Savior, the Lord Jesus Christ, and his determined, redemptive, absolutely saintly mother.

The final story occurred during the rededication of the Mexico City Mexico Temple in the fall of 2015. It was there with President Henry B. Eyring that I saw our beloved friend Lisa Tuttle Pieper stand in that moving dedicatory service. But she stood with some difficulty because with one arm she was holding up her beloved but severely challenged daughter, Dora, while with the other she was trying to manipulate Dora's dysfunctional right hand so this limited but eternally precious daughter of God could wave a white handkerchief and with groans intelligible only to herself and the angels of heaven cry out, "Hosanna, hosanna, hosanna to God and the Lamb" (see Joseph Smith, *History of the Church,* 2:427–28).

To mothers everywhere, past, present, or future, I say, "Thank you. Thank you for giving birth, for shaping souls, for forming character, and for demonstrating the pure love of Christ." To Mother Eve, to Sarah, Rebekah, and Rachel, to Mary of Nazareth, and to a Mother in Heaven* I say, "Thank you for your crucial role in fulfilling the purposes of eternity." To all mothers in every circumstance, including those who struggle—and all will—I say, "Be peaceful. Believe in God and yourself. You are doing better than you think you are. In fact, you are 'saviors on Mount Zion' (see Obadiah 1:21) and, like that of the Master you follow, your love 'never faileth'" (Moroni 7:46; 1 Corinthians 13:8). I can pay no higher tribute to anyone.

---

* See the recently published "Mother in Heaven" essay in LDS.org's *Gospel Topics* for the Church's doctrinal statement on this subject.

Motherhood: Finding Priority, Feeling Peace

PATRICIA T. HOLLAND

Before we ever blossom to the full fruition of our motherhood, we each wear a variety of faces in the different roles we play: teacher, confidante, caregiver, mentor, disciplinarian, healer, friend, to name just a few. Our countenances display charity, envy, patience, anxiety, pride, humility, generosity, greed, peace, perplexity. These portraits mirror joy and grief together, and through this exchange the lines are "woven fine." We are all learning of God's slow, steady way of sculpturing the experiences that cannot be escaped "till we have *our* face."

Which face is really yours? What is your role as a mother? What if the faces change so fast and the demands become so great that you hardly know who you are *any* of the time? How can you ever hope to be in control *all* of the time?

May I try to give some modest reassurances. First and most important, if we look closely in those many-mirrored faces, we will always see God's infinite care in the process of making us who we are and what we are becoming. We see the gentle way He kneels to brush back our hair or even to wipe away a tear. He adjusts the angle of the light and works His wonders with lines and scars and shadows. Ever so softly He whispers for us to endure difficulty or discouragement for what it may hold of illumination and eternal beauty. Under His hand our inner person becomes the outer person, and the artist shapes His perfect image.

While we participate in this process and reflect in sanctity and solitude, these perceptions and impressions of our relationship to our Father in Heaven can give us great peace and purpose. When we embrace these healing moments of worship, it is easier for us to keep this perspective and not succumb to the constant swirl of faces and roles and activities. With the complexities of rapid change in today's world, it is difficult to retain sight of our divine possibility or even to value our viability. In the rigorous demand of it all, we may wonder whether we can simply survive, let alone triumph.

We live in an enormously stressful world. Everyone seems to be either hurried or worried or both. News—both good and bad—travels fast, at the touch of a "share" button, and sorting out truth from error and important from trivial is ever more challenging in the Internet age. There are pressures of pacing ourselves with many time demands, and there seem to be increasing worries about what is expected of us, how much we should expect from ourselves, and how we can find the time, energy, and means to accomplish it all.

The scourge of our times is anxiety. Perhaps some of our anxiety comes, ironically, because the bounty and the blessings of our times have provided us as mothers with opportunities and choices our ancestors could never have considered. With automation and technology we have more discretionary time. With greater knowledge we are enjoying better health and more energy. And with more affluence we now have more opportunities to provide growth and special experiences for ourselves and our families. Our mothers and their mothers before them could not have dreamed of such freedom to choose, nor the abundance of such choices.

These blessings, however, add immensely to our anxiety when the choices we face suggest contention not only between right and wrong but, more often, between right and right. Should I carpool the kids to one more ballet lesson or take a class on "How to be a better mother"? Do

I spend the evening with my husband or do I run off to the chapel to hear the lecture on "What every man wants from his wife"? We worry and wonder if we should study to obtain more rewarding relationships or spend the needed time to cultivate them. And who comes first: our husband? our children? the Church? our extended family? our neighbors? nonmembers? our deceased ancestors? And what about ourselves?

Sometimes we know not where we should turn, nor which task should be done first. We feel frustrated, sometimes frightened, and often utterly fatigued. And too often we may feel like absolute failures. Where do we go for help? How do we stay fixed and focused? How do we stay centered and settled instead of floundering in a mindless mass of confusion? In short, how do we make order out of chaos?

I choose to believe that the Lord would not place us in this lone and dreary world without a blueprint for living. In Doctrine and Covenants 52:14 we read: "And again, I will give unto you a pattern in all things, that ye may not be deceived." He has given us patterns in the scriptures, and He has given us patterns in the temple ceremony.

I have chosen the patterns of the temple to share my own personal unveiling of the faces I have been asked to wear. I humbly pray that through my own intimate sharing, you may find a few threads of applicability as you search for your individual identity and eternal certainty.

The temple is highly symbolic. It has been called the university of the Lord. I find myself continually learning when I attend the temple with an expansive mind. I strive to exercise, to stretch, to look for deeper meaning. I look for parallels and symbols. I look for themes and motifs just as I would in a Bach or a Mozart composition, and I look for patterns—repeated patterns.

My habit of looking for sacred symbols and my testimony of finding answers to personal problems were passed on from mother to daughter to granddaughter to me. I have learned through generations of Eve's daughters the very close connection between our temporal challenges and the spiritual world, and how one assists the other as it pertains to those who attend the temple. So that you will understand my deep feelings about this, I have chosen to share my first experience about the temple's sustaining power.

I was twelve years old, living in Enterprise, Utah, when my parents were called to be temple workers in the St. George Utah Temple, fifty miles away. In telling me of their call, my mother spoke to me of what temples were, why people serve there, and what spiritual experiences some of the Saints have had there. Certainly she believed that the seen and unseen worlds meet and mingle in the temple. My duties were to get excused early from school once a week and hurry home to tend five unruly brothers, the youngest of whom was just a toddler. I remember complaining about this assignment one day,

17

and I will never forget the power with which my mother said, "When Daddy and I were set apart for this assignment, we were promised that our family would be blessed and protected, even by 'attending angels.'"

Late one afternoon on one of my parents' temple days, when I was feeling particularly exhausted from providing entertainment for my young charges, I put the baby in a buggy and, with the other boys, walked five blocks to visit with my grandmother.

After a warm greeting, Grandma suggested that we play on the lawn while she went to the store for refreshments. I was distracted with the other children and didn't notice the baby beginning to toddle after his grandmother. Suddenly, and with great fear, I realized that he was out of sight. Instinctively I ran toward the car just in time to see the back wheel turn completely over his small head, crushing it into the gravel beneath. In panic I screamed at the top of my lungs. My grandmother felt the distinct bump, heard my scream, and knew exactly what had happened. However, instead of stopping the car, she panicked and drove back over him again. Twice the wheel of the car moved completely over the head of this beloved baby brother for whom I had been given full responsibility.

The wailing of two hysterical voices quickly caught the attention of my grandfather. He dashed from the house and gathered up the baby (who my grandmother and I were sure was dead), and the three of them frantically drove fifty miles to the nearest doctor. I prayed and cried—cried and prayed. However, children remember promises made even when adults might forget, and I was curiously calm and comforted. I remembered the part about "attending angels."

After what seemed like an eternity, my grandparents called and reported that the baby was fine. He had a badly scratched face where the tire had scraped his head and cheek, but there was no cranial damage. Yet twice I had clearly seen the force of that wheel on his head.

At age twelve one cannot know many spiritual things. I especially did not know what went on in the temple of God. But I knew from *my* experience that it was sacred, and that hovering near, with approval and protection, were heavenly angels. I knew something of heavenly help beyond the veil.

In Doctrine and Covenants 109, that section which teaches us of the holiness of the temple, verse 22 reads: "We ask thee, Holy Father, that thy servants may go forth from this house armed with thy power, and that thy name may be upon them, and thy glory be round about them, and thine angels have charge over them."

That is a powerful promise to those who feel overwhelmed with the pressures and stresses of daily living, a power and promise I first encountered at twelve years of age. Now, with the many experiences I have had since that age, I can declare that this is true. The temple provides protection, and it provides patterns and promises that can settle and strengthen and stabilize us, however anxious our times. If we master the principles taught there, we will receive the promise the Lord gave us through Isaiah: "I will fasten him [or her] as a nail in a sure place" (Isaiah 23:23).

The Lord often allows us to wallow in mindless confusion before the teacher within us reveals the path that lightens our way. Jeff and I were young married graduate students with two babies and heavy Church assignments when President Harold B. Lee shared a prophet's counsel on "order in chaos." An anxious physician, worried that, because of his profession and Church responsibilities, he was neglecting his own son, asked President Lee, "How should I handle my time? What is most important in life? How do I do it all?" President Lee replied, "A man's first responsibility is to himself, then to his family, then to the Church, realizing that we have responsibilities to excel in our professions as well." He then stressed that a man must first take care of his own health, both physically and emotionally, before he can be a blessing to others.

As a young mother I wrestled with this counsel, considering carefully how one taking care of herself first manages to lose herself for others. As the years passed, I saw how the truth in President Lee's counsel seemed to fit perfectly the order spoken of in the temple. The temple teaches priorities, it teaches order, it teaches growth, it teaches joy and fulfillment. Consider the following teachings from the temple (I have taken the words from the scriptures so that I will not inappropriately trifle with sacred things).

In the fourth chapter of Abraham, the Gods plan the creation of the earth and all life thereon. In these plans (which take thirty-one verses to outline), the word or a form of the word *order* is used sixteen times. The Gods organize and give order to every living thing. "And the Gods said: We will do everything that we have said, and organize them; and they will become very obedient" (Abraham 4:31). If we are to become like the Gods, we will begin with order. We will choose to obey the laws and principles of heaven that lead to order.

One of the first truths taught in the temple is that every living thing shall fill "the measure of its creation" (see D&C 88:19). That is a powerful commandment! Consider it in light of President Lee's counsel. I must admit that when I first heard this directive I thought it meant only procreation: having issue, bearing offspring. I am sure that is the most important part of its meaning, but much of the temple ceremony is symbolic, so surely there are multiple meanings in that statement as well. How else does a woman fill the measure of her creation? How does she become all that her heavenly parents intend her to be? Growth, fulfillment, reaching, stretching, and developing our talents are part of the process of becoming like God, the ultimate "measure of our creation."

How can we be fully successful wives or mothers or missionaries or temple workers or citizens or neighbors if we are not trying to bring our best self to these tasks? Surely that is why we need to be strong physically and emotionally in order to help others be strong. That is the order of creation.

Online and in print, we are constantly reminded that proper diet, appropriate exercise, and plenty of rest increase our daily capacities as well as our life span. But all too many of us put off even these minimal efforts, thinking our family, our neighbors, and our other many responsibilities come first. Yet in doing so, we put at risk the thing these people need most from us: our healthiest, happiest, heartiest self. When they ask for bread, let us not be so weary and unhealthy that we give them a stone.

The issue for me, then, is accepting that we are worth the time and effort it takes to achieve the full measure of our creation, and believing that it is not selfish, wrong, or evil. It is, in fact, essential to our spiritual development.

My oldest child tried to teach me this

principle many years ago. I had not been feeling well on a day I had promised to take this then three-year-old son to the zoo. As my aches and pains increased, I finally said in exasperation, "Matthew, I don't know if we should go to the zoo and take care of you or if we should stay home and take care of Mother." He looked up at me for a moment with his big brown eyes and then stated emphatically, "Mama, I think *you* should take care of *you*, so *you* can take care of *me*." He was wise enough even at that age to know where his best interests were ultimately served. Unless we take care of ourselves, it's virtually impossible to properly take care of others.

Medical experts are confirming, from studying people who are overworried as well as overworked, that many illnesses are stress related. Therefore, the basic questions to ask while selflessly serving others are, How much tension in our lives is too much? When does it become counterproductive? Jennifer James, formerly of the psychiatry department at the University of Washington, gives us some suggestions:

"Everyone needs a certain amount of body tension. It keeps us upright. But how much is too much? Have you checked your body lately? How are you feeling? How about your neck—how stiff is it? Or your shoulders? Can you find your balance? Are you centered? Are you irritable? Have you yelled at anyone lately? How about your stomach? Your stomach will always tell you the truth, unless you give it antacid and teach it to lie. We know how to tell that we're tense, but we sometimes ignore it. The question is, why?

"We know that exercise gives almost instant relief from tension. We know that if we give up caffeine and sugar, stop smoking, and give up being workaholics we can relieve stress. But we don't choose to.

"Some people think that someone else will take the responsibility—their parents, their friends, their spouse, maybe even Mother Nature.

But if you don't take care of yourself, no one else will. What is your choice? Why are you choosing not to take care of your stresses? Do you think that you don't deserve to feel better? You do" (*Success Is the Quality of Your Journey* [1986], 23).

Our physician scolded me one day during an examination when he noted that the lowest thing on my list of concerns was caring for myself. He looked me sternly in the eye and asked me to remember the promises made in the endowment, and then he asked me to think about the promises of the initiatory ordinances. Our children and our children's children and all of our posterity depend in some measure upon our physical health. Caring for our physical health is, then, a prerequisite to emotional health.

We have been created to become like the Gods. That means we already have inherent within us godly attributes, the greatest of which is Christlike charity. And the key to emotional health is charity—love. Joy comes from loving and being loved. When this divine attribute is at work in our feelings for our family, our neighbors, our God, *and ourselves,* we feel joy. When it is immobilized with conflict toward others, toward God, or toward ourselves, we are depressed in our growth and we become depressed in our attitude.

Depression, conflict, or negativism is often a message to us that we are not growing toward the full measure for which God has created us. Our pain—emotional pain—is a demand that we stop and take time for change in our life because we may be getting off course. As Elder Richard L. Evans used to say, "What's the use of running if you are on the wrong road?" Of course, we all get on the wrong road occasionally; we all have conflicts and discouragement and make mistakes sometimes. But I love this thought from Sister Teres Lizia: "If you are willing to serenely bear the trial of [personal disappointment and weakness] then you will be for Jesus a pleasant place of shelter." The key word is *serene*. If we bear our weaknesses and mistakes, hurt feelings and misgivings, *serenely*, and if we accept the down times and learn from them, they will pass and return less often.

We receive mixed messages today that self-love and a sense of self-worth are forms of selfishness and conceit. However, I know from my own experience that when I don't fully accept myself and all of my warts, blemishes, and imperfections, I am crippled in my charity toward God and my neighbors. Let me encourage you not to feel guilty as you aspire to appropriate self-love, which comes in part by honest self-knowledge and acceptance.

Perhaps we all agree on this premise, yet we are unsure about the process for achieving it. It is easier for me to understand when I see it applied to someone other than myself. For example, I begin to love my neighbor when I create experiences that will allow me to get to know her and understand why she acts and reacts the way she does in different circumstances and settings. The more I know her, the more I understand her. And the more I understand her, the more I love her. My knowledge of God also increases when I spend more time with Him in prayer, in His holy writ, and in His service. And the more I know and understand Him, the more I love Him.

This same principle applies to ourselves. Appropriately loving ourselves requires looking within ourselves deeply, honestly, and, as Sister Teres suggests, serenely. It requires a loving look at the bad as well as the good. The more we understand and know, the more we love.

Our Father in Heaven needs us as we are, as we are growing to become. He has intentionally made us different from one another so that even with our imperfections we can fulfill His purposes. My greatest misery comes when I feel I have to fit what others are doing, or what I think others expect of me. I am most happy when I am comfortable being me and trying to do what my Father in Heaven and I expect me to do.

For many years I tried to measure the oft-times quiet, reflective, thoughtful Pat Holland against the robust, bubbly, talkative, and energetic Jeff Holland and others with like qualities. I have learned through several fatiguing failures that you can't have joy in being bubbly if you are not a bubbly person. It is a contradiction in terms. I have given up seeing myself as a flawed person because my energy level is lower than Jeff's, and I don't talk as much as he does, nor as fast. Giving this up has freed me to embrace and rejoice in my own manner and personality in the measure of *my* creation. Ironically, that has allowed me to admire and enjoy Jeff's ebullience even more.

Somewhere, somehow the Lord "blipped the message onto my screen" that my personality was created to fit precisely the mission and talents He gave me. For example, the quieter, calmer talent of playing the piano reveals much about the real Pat Holland. I would never have learned to play the piano if I hadn't enjoyed the long hours of solitude required for its development. This same principle applies to my love of writing, reading, meditation, and especially teaching and talking with my children. Miraculously, I have found that I have untold abundant sources of energy to be myself. But the moment I indulge in imitation of my neighbor, I feel fractured and fatigued and find myself forever swimming upstream. When we frustrate God's plan for us, we deprive this world and God's kingdom of our unique contributions, and a serious schism settles in our soul. God never gave us any task beyond our ability to accomplish it. We just have to be willing to do it our own way. We will always have enough resources for being who we are and what we can become.

Self-knowledge is not selfish; it is a priority spiritual journey. Paul exhorts, "Examine yourselves, whether ye be in the faith; prove your own selves. Know ye not your own selves, how that Jesus Christ is in you?" (2 Corinthians 13:5). We must each prepare right now to intensify our own inner journey. In no other structure—in no other setting—can we receive more illuminating light shining on our self-realization than in the temple. As we go there often, the Lord will teach us that we have been created that we might have joy, and joy comes as we embrace the true measure of our creation.

In the Doctrine and Covenants we read: "Do thou grant, Holy Father, that all those who shall worship in this house may be taught words of wisdom . . . and that they may grow up in thee, and receive a fulness of the Holy Ghost, and be organized according to thy laws, and be prepared to obtain every needful thing" (D&C 109:14–15).

After our physical and emotional health, our next priority is family, and a Latter-day Saint family begins where it ends: with a man and a woman, united in the temple of the Lord. In the temple we come to understand that "neither is the man without the woman, neither the woman without the man, in the Lord" (1 Corinthians

11:11). Abraham 4:27 reads: "So the Gods went down to organize man in their own image, in the image of the Gods to form they him, male and female to form they them." It takes both male and female to make the complete image of God.

When we were married more than fifty years ago, Jeff and I became a new entity. Together, Jeff, with all of his maleness, and I, with all of my femaleness, create a complete and unfragmented new whole. When we are integrated, Jeff shares in my femininity and I share in his masculinity so that the whole, fitly joined together, is much greater than the sum of the parts. But Satan does not want us to be one. He knows that the marital body in its unity and wholeness has great power, and he insidiously insists upon independence, individuation, and autonomy. So eventually the body is fragmented—broken.

May I share a thought from Madeleine L'Engle: "The original relationship between male and female was meant to be one of mutual fulfillment and joy, but that relationship was broken, to our grief, and turned into one of suspicion and warfare, misunderstanding and exclusion, and will not be fully restored until the end of time. Nevertheless, we are given enough glimpses of the original relationship so that we should be able to rejoice in our participation" (*The Irrational Season* [1977], 9).

A perspective I keep in mind that helps maintain oneness for Pat and Jeff Holland is that we come together as equal, whole, developing, and contributing partners. Most of our movement together is in a lateral relationship. We move side by side, together, simultaneously, much like double-yoked oxen. But there are times when, for the sake of godly progress and development, I follow my husband in a vertical relationship. A house of God is a house of order. We all fall in line behind someone in that straight course that leads to eternal bliss. I am so grateful that I fall in line with Jeff (and he tells me he's more than happy to fall in line with me).

If God created us to be one together, we

must be number one for each other. "But from the beginning God made them male and female. For this cause shall a man leave his father and mother, and cleave to his wife; and they twain shall be one flesh" (Mark 10:6–8).

I firmly believe that my husband comes first—before friends, father, mother, community, Church, even children. We were together, alone, in the beginning of our marriage, and, heaven willing, we will be together in the end. Fortunately I think we have both been mature enough to realize when the children's needs have superseded our own, but our grown children now concede that the best thing we ever did for them, the greatest security they enjoyed, was our loving of and caring for each other.

When our daughter, Mary, was about nine years old, she sensitively noticed that both Jeff and I were looking a little frazzled and frayed around the edges and so pronounced, "Mother, it's that time again. Take Daddy and go away together." The children recognize that our time together is one of the most restoring, redeeming things we can do for them as well as for ourselves.

I love the Lord's injunction to Emma Smith—even to all wives: "The office of thy calling shall be for a comfort unto my servant, . . . thy husband, in his afflictions, with consoling words, in the spirit of meekness" (D&C 25:5). I feel that I am at the pinnacle of my creation when I am comforting and consoling my husband. Nothing is more rewarding or brings me more joy. The sweetest sounds I hear are spoken when Jeff whispers to me, "You are my anchor, my foundation, my reassurance. I could never do this job without you."

And I love equally Paul's counsel to *all* husbands: "So ought men to love their wives as their own bodies. He that loveth his wife loveth himself, for no man ever yet hated his own flesh; but nourisheth and cherisheth it, even as the Lord the church: for we are members of his body, of his flesh, and of his bones" (Ephesians 5:28–30).

Second, marriages are formed to procreate, to bring forth a posterity—having joy and rejoicing therein. A crucial part of any priority in a marriage, then, is children, even as I readily acknowledge that some couples have not been blessed with that opportunity. Indeed, most of my anxiety in life has centered on my children and grandchildren. Since the world I live in is so full of complexities and challenges, I fear and tremble occasionally as I anticipate theirs. We are already seeing signs of their times. Enoch saw visions of their future; he saw their troubles and tribulations; he saw "men's hearts failing them, looking forth with fear" (see Moses 7:58–69).

Jeff and I both agree that after our own effort toward individual and marital spirituality, our greatest spiritual priority is conscientious, devoted parenthood, to see that our children "shall not be afraid of evil tidings; [that their] hearts [are] fixed, trusting in the Lord" (Psalm 112:7). We have determined that our children will be peaceful, fixed, and trusting in the Lord—in large part at least—only so far as their parents are peaceful, fixed, and trusting in the Lord. I believe that the most powerful influence in a child's life is imitation, especially imitation of a parent. If we are hurried and worried or unbalanced in any way, surely our children will be hurried, worried, and unbalanced.

To live calmly and reassuringly for our children requires time—peaceful, loving, centered time. This means learning how to say no to some of the other demands that come along, without feeling guilty. I haven't learned yet how to do everything, but with the incredible practice I have had over the years, I have become an expert in saying no without feeling guilty. Jeff and I have counseled together, and we have always tried to set aside appropriately proportioned time for ourselves, each other, our family, our Church responsibilities, and our community. That is a lot to try to juggle.

So I have learned to say no to some things

in order to be able to say yes to others. The most important yes we can say to our children is, "Yes, I have time for you." And for me that means both quantity and quality time.

I had two wonderful years serving full-time as a counselor in the Young Women general presidency of the Church. For many reasons I am grateful the Lord called me out of the home for those two years of service. I was able to contribute to the lives of children who may not have the advantages we enjoy in our home. At the same time, my husband and children learned the importance of sacrifice and of serving each other, and the joy of knowing Christ will compensate and carry us when we are called according to His purposes.

Having a full-time opportunity outside of the home also taught me something of the challenges that are created when trying to juggle family and the expectations of the workplace. Contributing people, by their own success, work themselves into a position of more obligation. As my months of service continued, I began to see the mushrooming effect of those demands running headlong into my responsibilities as a wife and parent. As Deborah Fallows has written, "The more 'successful' the position is, in terms of prestige, power, money, and responsibility, the more commonplace and restricting its tyranny can be" (*A Mother's Work* [1985], 18–19). It is easier to ask our children to yield to the demands of our schedule than to ask an employer to do so. Children haven't yet learned to speak up for their needs.

Of course, every family's situation is different, and thus every couple bears the responsibility to counsel with the Lord about how best to provide for their family's needs. There should be no judgment between us on such matters. One important principle remains the same, however, regardless of our circumstances: Children need time. We need to trust the Lord to inspire us and give us opportunities to be there for them at crucial points.

For example, one afternoon my daughter, Mary, came home from school a little earlier than usual. Now, if I had been at Church headquarters in Salt Lake City, as I often was during that period, I wouldn't have been home to receive her, but that day the Lord positioned me where I was needed most. She entered the kitchen in tears about a conversation she had had with friends and a teacher over some controversial and disturbing issues. This led to the warmest, most intimate and enlightening experience we had ever had in her teen years, enough so that it prompted her to say, "You know, Mom, if you hadn't been home, we never would have had this conversation because I wouldn't have felt the need after a peanut butter sandwich and a little TV."

Since the conversation had to do with virtues and values that are incredibly important, I have thanked the Lord frequently for just that one moment. Our best quality moments with our children often come *not* when we're prepared and trying to have them, but as surprising, fleeting episodes that we couldn't have anticipated. We need to ask the Lord to help us be there to catch those moments.

Being away from my children for long hours over two years helped me to understand that when one or more of my children are overwhelmed or confused or struggling, there is a distinct way that I will respond as their mother—different from how a babysitter, friend, or even their grandmother, however loving or confident she may be, would respond. Ironically, it was through my full-time service to a Church program that I learned fully to appreciate that no one else can mother my children as well as I can, and that my greatest task and joy is as a wife and mother in my own home.

Noted psychologist Scott Peck has written: "The parents who devote time to their children even when it is not demanded by glaring misdeeds will perceive in them subtle needs for discipline, to which they will respond with gentle urging or reprimand or structure or praise, administered with thoughtfulness and care. They will observe how their children eat cake, how they study, when they tell subtle falsehoods, when they run away from problems rather than face them. They will take the time to make these minor corrections and adjustments, listening to their children, responding to them, tightening a little here, loosening a little there, giving them little lectures, little stories, little hugs and kisses, little admonishments, little pats on the back" (*The Road Less Traveled* [1978], 23).

Essential to every child's mental health is the feeling, "I am valuable." And where we choose to spend our time reveals to our children exactly how valuable they are. In this way, children provide parents their greatest spiritual development. Our children are our practice in being eternal parents.

The final priority in our spirituality has to do with building the kingdom of God. I always try to remember that all of our major priorities are related, that the Church is an earthly structure provided to help me in my eternal responsibility to my God, my family, and those others upon whom I can have righteous influence, living or dead. The Church helps me so much in those tasks that I am more than willing to take my turn, to play my part in helping others in their progress.

Of course, the Lord knows that our Church service, besides blessing and helping others, increases our own personal development. I fully acknowledge that because of my Church service, I have begun to develop talents I wasn't sure were there—talents of speaking, writing, teaching, music, learning, and especially loving. Above all, the Church provides a structure for developing the godly attribute of charity that I need so much as a mother.

Sometimes choosing between family and church is the most difficult of all the choices we face. But here, too, our prophets have given guidelines for deciding what is essential and what is secondary. When every home is patterned after the order of the temple—"even a house of prayer, a house of fasting, a house of faith, a house of learning, a house of glory, a house of order, a house of God" (D&C 109:8)—the kingdom of God will come. But since neither we nor our homes are yet perfect, and because many are yet pioneering with less privilege than some others have had, we extend ourselves through the structure and programs of the Church to teach, bless, serve, and sacrifice for others who are not in our own family until we are equal in all things. We are all blessed immeasurably for our service in the Church. It is the most beneficial way we have to keep the two great commandments: to love God and our neighbors as we love ourselves.

Let me end just as I began, by coming full circle. In a very personal way I have shared my perspective of the organization and order that the teachings of the temple have provided for me, but not with the idea that your life should be exactly like Pat Holland's, for each of us will have peace only as we are filling the measure of our *own* creation. My prayer is merely that I have been able to trigger your thought processes for establishing priorities for your own life. My hope is that this message will create in each of us a desire to mentally mark out our purpose in life so that we will not fall easy prey to petty worries, fears, and weaknesses, or to temporary failures, setbacks, and unhappiness. You see, like you, I have those wonderful days when I wake up feeling warm, cozy, with feelings of purpose and peace that all is well. But dynamic tensions are at work in each of us. Burdens of mystery, divine discontent, and inner turmoil keep us from complacency, creating Christlike energy searching for new truth.

On those days when I feel off center, out of focus, or off balance, when I feel that I don't have enough time, insight, or strength to solve my problems, I know that comfort is as close as the temple. Before I go to the temple, I retreat to a private room in my home, one where, from frequent prayer, I feel I have come closest to my Father in Heaven. There I kneel and express my deepest feelings of love and gratitude. I also pour out my troubles to Him one by one by one, laying every burden and placing every decision at the Lord's feet. Thus prepared, I then take myself out of this world of fashion, frenzy, and occasional phoniness and go to the house of the Lord. There, dressed like my neighbor, and with no windows and no clocks to distract me, I am able to see this world objectively. There I remember that the whole of this life is a journey of the spirit to a higher and holier sphere. I remember that the success of my journey depends on my adherence to the sequential steps God has put on my individual road map.

While serving another sister in the temple, someone who didn't have my privileges during her lifetime, I have time for solitude, private prayer, and meditation. I have time to listen and to contemplate the steps I can take, those steps that are right for me. The Lord often shows me how to effectively make choices between right and wrong—and between right and right. He blesses me to see what is essential and what is secondary. I feel comforted regarding my discouragements, and I am able to see those moments as merely messages guiding me back toward my own individual divine destiny. If the Lord in His love and graciousness does that for me, I bear you my testimony that He will also do that for you!

We are children of heavenly parents who have invited us on a journey to become like them. They have provided for us, just a shadow away, a sacred home where we can go and remember that there is joy in this journey, that our paths do have a purpose, and that life can be lived as lovingly on earth as it is in heaven. May we strive to reflect that radiant spirit of the Lord and that love in all we do.

A TIME FOR MOTHERS

JEFFREY R. HOLLAND
PATRICIA T. HOLLAND

SISTER HOLLAND: The scriptural story of Esther marks the convergence of an important woman with an important moment, an important "time." We want to focus here on *our time,* what this time is, and how we, the mothers of the Church, can seize it, Esther-like, to turn it to advantage.

ELDER HOLLAND: First of all, may I say this is a time to be grateful and optimistic. Ours is the most blessed, the most abundant and glorious time in the history of the world. We really do mean "fulness" when we speak of the dispensation of the fulness of times. We have more blessings spread among more people in more parts of the world than ever before in the story of the human family.

SISTER HOLLAND: And, of course, as Latter-day Saints, the way we can make things better and better for our children—and for everyone—is to share our love and share the principles, covenants, and promises of the gospel of Jesus Christ. To have had the gospel restored in our time, for our benefit and that of our children and our grandchildren, is the greatest of all the blessings of our time. We have so much to share.

ELDER HOLLAND: I have often told young people that for the privilege of living in such a time they (we) have a responsibility that has never come in exactly this way to any other dispensation of Church members. We are the people in the eternal scheme of things who must prepare the Church of the Lamb for the arrival of the Lamb. No earlier people in ancient days ever had that assignment. What a tremendous responsibility! This means that before this is over we have to look like His Church members would look and act like His Church members would act. This will require all of us to move closer and closer to the heart of the gospel, to true principles of discipleship and faith, qualities of the heart and spirit. In short, it means we have to live and be, to actually demonstrate, what it is we are always so quick to say we "know" in our testimony meetings. Eventually that has to mean not so much of programs or external schedules and certainly not so much of temporal things or the distractions the world puts before us. As a people we must increasingly strive for inner qualities, striving for profound faith and deep spirituality, striving to live as disciples of Christ would live. That is the task for us and for our families in this time of "dispensational hastening."

SISTER HOLLAND: Sisters, we especially want you to hear our great desire to pass the blessings of the gospel—and especially the love of the gospel—on to the next generation—our children and grandchildren and yours. In that spirit, may I share a very personal story with you. My great-grandmother on my mother's side of the family came from the Bern-Interlaken area of Switzerland. You may have visited there, or at least seen the travel posters! Surely it is among the most beautiful locations on the face of the earth—green and majestic nature at its loveliest.

After joining the Church and emigrating to join the Saints moving west, those great-grandparents were called to settle the little community of Enterprise in southern Utah. Perhaps you have been to Enterprise, too, but I know you have not seen any travel posters of it! I do love the community of my birth and childhood memories, but it is not Switzerland! It was hot in the summer and cold in the winter, the wind blew constantly, and it was barren. What a test of faith it must have been for these Swiss ancestors to be called to such an area so totally opposite to that green land of lakes and alpine beauty they had left behind!

My great-grandmother decided she would do something about it. With her two hands and a shovel, she harvested some small pine tree seedlings from the mountains not far away and planted them around the small church building that had just been erected. Then every day she would carry two buckets of water from her home nearly three blocks away, one bucket in each hand, to water those trees and keep them growing. It was arduous work for a little woman bent over with osteoporosis, but she made every drop count in a daily ritual that over time gave each tree a regular, if meager, drink of moisture.

ELDER HOLLAND: In this exercise Pat's great-grandmother often took her little ten-year-old granddaughter with her, telling stories and reminiscing about her life in Switzerland as she carried her two precious buckets of water. One day one of the brethren of the community stopped her and said, with something of a dismissive tone, "Oh, Sister Barlocker, why do you make this useless journey each day to water those scrubby little pine trees? They will never survive in this harsh climate and difficult soil, and even if they did, they will never grow to any size in your lifetime. Why don't you just give up and forget your high Swiss hopes in this matter?"

Well, little Sister Barlocker rose to the full four feet eight inches of her stature, looked this good brother in the eye, and said, "I know these trees will not grow very large in my lifetime. But if I stay with it, they will live and they will grow. And although I will not enjoy their beauty and their shade, this little girl will. I am doing this for her."

SISTER HOLLAND: That ten-year-old grandchild was my mother. And my mother, with all of her siblings, and cousins, and everyone else in Enterprise did live to see those trees reach an impressive height and give off lovely, much-needed shade from the desert sun. Then I grew up enjoying those trees, playing under their branches, and seeing them frame the church I attended as a young woman. And now I have lived to see not only my children but also my grandchildren play, have picnics, laugh, and hold 24th of July relay races all through and in and around those beautiful trees, which now literally tower over the community—and over the pioneer heritage—of little windblown, once-barren Enterprise, Utah.

In this homely little story my great-grandmother taught me several wonderful lessons.

First, speaking of a time for gratitude, I am so grateful that she did something for her posterity that was hard and demanding, but that she knew would bless their lives and bring them happiness. And of course, that wasn't just planting lovely trees. That faithful mother taught her children and her grandchildren the gospel, lived it every day of her life, and brought pure, uncompromised righteousness to us in a way that none of her posterity could ever deny. In that sense she nourished us even more faithfully than she nourished those trees!

I pray we will all live with this sense of linked generations. In a very real way, my grandmother did what she did *for me,* and that helps me want to do what I do for my children and grandchildren, for generations yet to come, so that they will be blessed in the gospel and have privileges in their lives that I may not see but that they will.

Thinking about all of this, including my husband's comments about preparing the Church of the Lamb for the return of the Lamb, has given me a new insight into the scripture in the Doctrine and Covenants that says, "For thus saith the Lord, I will cut my work short in righteousness" (D&C 52:11). I have always thought that meant that the Lord wouldn't let wickedness go on too long, that He would "cut the last days short" rather than allow too much damage to be done. I am sure it does mean something of that, but lately I have wondered if it didn't also mean that the work can be cut short—or finished—only if there is a clear demonstration of righteousness among the Saints, only if we are looking and acting not only like the Church of the Lamb but like the Lamb Himself! Maybe it is a little like the change that comes when hot water turns to steam. We can sort of move along as reasonably warm-water people, but until we push it to that magic 100 degrees centigrade we don't get the miracle of change that a burst of steam offers. Maybe this is just my own interpretation of this scripture about "cut[ting the] work short in righteousness," but if a little more righteousness can cut these last days a little shorter and bring the Savior's return a little sooner, I am all for it!

ELDER HOLLAND: One of the great truths Pat expressed in that wonderful little story of her great-grandmother is that bringing forward this day of righteousness, a day that will make the members of the Church what we ought to be, requires us to focus on the children. We don't know when the Lord will "cut short" His work, but we know that the coming generations—our children and grandchildren, collectively speaking—move progressively toward it, whenever it is, and they must be as prepared for that day as we are trying to be—or even more so. So this truly is a time for mothers—a time when a mother's righteous influence becomes ever more necessary.

SISTER HOLLAND: I have always loved this verse from Alma, who said to his children: "And now, . . . this [is] the ministry unto which ye were called, to declare these glad tidings unto this people, to prepare their minds; . . . that they may prepare the minds of their children to hear the word at the time of his coming" (Alma 39:16).

And may I say you mothers are doing a wonderful job of that. As we travel around the Church we see magnificent children and youth—Primary children who carry their scriptures to church and teenagers who can't wait to go on missions and marry in the temple. The

Lord loves you for what you are doing in preparing the minds and the hearts of His children. And we love you too!

ELDER HOLLAND: Dear sisters, our beloved associates in this work, in "such a time as this" may I plead with you never to underestimate or undervalue your divine role both as personal, powerful contributors to the kingdom of God and as the nurturers and benefactors of His "little ones," who will yet have such a divine impact on the unfolding of this work. As President Russell M. Nelson has said, "We need women who know how to make important things happen by their faith and who are courageous defenders of morality and families in a sin-sick world. We need women who are devoted to shepherding God's children along the covenant path toward exaltation; women who know how to receive personal revelation, who understand the power and peace of the temple endowment; women who know how to call upon the powers of heaven to protect and strengthen children and families; women who teach fearlessly" (*Ensign*, Nov. 2015, 96).

I fear that virtually nothing—or at least not much—that the world says to you acknowledges your divine role as women. I am reminded that throughout the Creation sequence of Genesis God viewed His work, including the creation of man, and called it "good." But for the one and only time in that Creation story He then said something was "not good." He said it was not good that man should be alone. In short the Creation, even with Adam, was incomplete. Here I invoke President Gordon B. Hinckley's language:

"As His final creation, the crowning of His glorious work, He created woman. I like to regard Eve as His masterpiece after all that had gone before, the final [great] work before He rested from His labors" (*Ensign*, Nov. 1991, 97). I join my testimony to President Hinckley's in that assessment. Surely it must have been at this point, with so much that was "good" having been done and having remedied the one thing that was "not good," He could say after Eve's arrival it was all "very good" (Genesis 1:31).

In this great, eternal work, mothers have carried the torch of faith and family from the beginning. The need for that torch to burn brightly and dispel darkness has never been greater than "in this time." Little wonder that the Prophet Joseph said, "If you live up to your privileges, the angels cannot be restrained from being your associates" (*History of the Church,* 4:605). The scriptures speak of women being "elect." What a powerful doctrinal and covenantal term! And who "elects" you? You do!—and so does God Himself, who has all the joy and delight of a father in you as His daughter, you who pass on light and hope, pass on life itself and a glorious gospel legacy until the work is finished.

SISTER HOLLAND: In all of this, we do not want you to feel overwhelmed. If the work of true righteousness yet before us seems monumental, remember that we have monumental help. We, as women, have too often thought we are "little" people with little influence, but the Lord keeps pleading with us not to think that way, not when we are His divine daughters on His errand. As the Lord said, "Wherefore, as ye are agents, ye are on the Lord's errand; and whatever ye do according to the will of the Lord is the Lord's business" (D&C 64:29).

Mothers have the commission to create, to bring to fruition and provide development of the divinity within the children of God. With that commission comes a divine spiritual capacity that (to me) is unfathomable to our human view. Some of the words that come to my mind regarding a woman's discipleship are life, love, energy, holiness, intelligence, strength, change.

ELDER HOLLAND: Sisters, we all need to believe in ourselves as God's "agents" much, much more than we do, activating the gifts and the powers He has given us as if He Himself were here. On the outside we may seem to be "little" people, little everyday souls with everyday problems, but we are the everyday instruments God has always used to do His work and perform His miracles from the beginning. This is that power of the Atonement to which we pay much too little attention—not only did Christ save us from our sins but He saved us from ourselves, our horrible warped opinions and negative views of ourselves. That is the miracle of being reborn and "spiritually begotten of [the Savior]," as King Benjamin said, of saying that we are "changed through faith on his name" (Mosiah 5:7). If we say we are "changed through faith on his name," then let's act like such a change has occurred.

SISTER HOLLAND: I want to add here that all of us need to remember we are more divine than we are temporal, and only the adversary would have us believe otherwise. Remember we are truly spiritual beings having a short temporal experience. If we can remember that, we can more readily call upon those spiritual gifts that are ours and that have been made powerful in us through the Atonement of Christ. I read a poet recently who wrote of the "consuming fire of Christ," a divine flame that would burn away our sins and shortcomings, our sorrows and inadequacies. That is something I want to pass on to the next generation—"the consuming fire of Christ"—a fire set by our own love.

In that spirit, may I say that one of my great wishes is that ours will be a time when we stop "beating up" on ourselves and let the grace of heaven wash over us and make us whole—truly "holy." Remember, no matter what you have done, you can be forgiven of it, so get the process started by forgiving yourself and let repentance lead you on to the miracle of God's forgiveness. Take hope. Look up. Be good to yourself, because your Heavenly Father surely wants to be good to you. Let's let the Spirit envelop us, make us calm, and heal our souls.

ELDER HOLLAND: Knowing mothers as I do, I want to say to you, "No, everything you have done is not wrong. No, you are not a failure. No, you are not personally to blame for every mishap in the world since the ark landed." We are all pretty hard on ourselves, but it seems to me women are harder on themselves than men will ever be. Why is that so? We ask you not to do it. Repent when or where that is necessary, but then honor that other "R"—Rejoice! Make a resolve today that this is "your time" to be good to yourself. It will surprise you how much that helps you be good to all the others whom you want so much to bless in your life.

SISTER HOLLAND: Sisters, may I make an appeal that it is a time for us, especially as mothers, to try to strip ourselves of something else that also seems so prevalent among women. I suppose men suffer with such things, too, but it seems to be particularly evident, and particularly painful, among mothers. It is closely related to the things my husband just touched on. I speak of the constant feeling we seem to have that what we are or what we have is not enough. That is Satan's demonic chant sounding continually in our ears. It is not true! We are more intelligent than this. We are stronger, much stronger, than this! Constantly comparing ourselves with others—a habit made frighteningly possible by the Internet—leaves us feeling so weak and worthless. It taps into our pride and poisons with jealousy. Let's start a new "chant"—that we are women of Christ, that we are spiritually strong personally, and that we will prepare the next generation for their opportunities. Let us strip ourselves of pride and vanity and envy forever.

Listen to this counsel given in ancient days. It is very direct concerning what we, as sisters in this Church, ought to address. Alma asks: "Behold, are ye stripped of pride? I say unto you, if ye are not ye are not prepared to meet God. . . .

"Behold, I say, is there one among you who is not stripped of envy? I say unto you that such an one is not prepared; and I would that he [and she!] should prepare quickly, for the hour is close at hand, and [she] knoweth not when the time shall come" (Alma 5:28–29).

May I stress that this stripping ourselves of envy and pride is a poignant, almost painful description of what we must be willing to do. Furthermore, when we have undergone such a potentially painful "stripping" of an adverse trait, we must then help our daughters and grand-daughters and the young women who come under our influence (and the men!) do the same. Heaven only knows how much the world uses envy and pride and worldly glamour in our society. We have to walk away from these things, but this will not be easy to do. We will need those gifts of heaven of which we spoke earlier, the power of God's grace and priesthood, the atoning power of the Savior, which compensates where we try and try but seem to fall short.

James knew all this. He said: "The spirit which God implanted in us [all of us] turns to-wards envious desires. Yet the grace he gives is stronger. Thus the scripture says, God opposes the arrogant and gives grace to the humble. Be submissive then to God. . . . Come close to

[him] and he will come close to you. . . . Humble yourselves before God and he will lift you up" (James 4:5–6, 8, 10, New English Bible).

Isn't that a tremendous thought? If we would not "lift" ourselves up with these cursed temptations of envy and pride, God would gladly step in and do the "lifting" for us! Only He can lift us up where He wants us and where we really want to be. We can't get there by clawing or clamor, by cattiness or cutting others down. We certainly can't get there by vaunting ourselves "up."

Furthermore I believe with all my heart that this is a challenge we will face again and again. We should not be discouraged if the challenge returns tomorrow just when we thought we gave it such a good effort today. I say this out of the honesty, and experience, of my own heart. I struggle with these issues just as you do, and just as everyone does. So don't give up hope— and don't think you are the only one who feels these things or struggles with these temptations. We all do, but every effort is a godly one, and every victory is counted for our good. And if we turn around to face the same challenge again tomorrow, so be it. We will work again, with all our heart, to strip away anything that keeps us from truly being "meek and lowly"—in all the right ways—before God. His grace is sufficient to help us succeed at that.

My dear sisters and friends, collectively speaking, I think about you all the time. I love you. I know most of you have experienced some heartache and disappointment as well as joy and hopefulness. We have wanted our words to be encouraging to you and that you would recognize in them our love for you. I truly believe that "cut[ting the] work short in righteousness" requires the element of love to prevail in our lives. Love of God, love of each other, and, yes, love of ourselves. The two great commandments are still the two great commandments. These will be the ultimate marks of our discipleship. The sooner we can come to that love, the sooner we are truly Christ's people and (to my mind) the sooner He can come. If we can do this, live with true, expansive charity and unbounded love, perhaps our children will then see our example and recognize that we, their mothers and grand-mothers, their aunts and sisters, their teachers and the wonderful women in this Church, are disciples of the Savior of the world—because we have "love one to another" (John 13:34–35). My earnest prayer is that we can receive His image in our countenance and sing "the song of re-deeming love" (Alma 5:26) forever in this, His true and redeeming Church.

ELDER HOLLAND: Pat has testified of our need to increase love in our discipleship. Let my testi-mony be the other half of hers, to testify how much the Father and the Son personify love and shower it upon our sometimes meager efforts to do the same. I believe if you could grasp in some small way the vision of Their majestic love for you, it would free you to love Them and every-one else within your circle of influence in pro-found and powerful new ways. One of the most important verses I know of in all of scripture is the supplication Jesus gave in the great intercessory prayer prior to His suffering in Gethsemane and Crucifixion on Golgotha. In that prayer, the Savior said, "And this is life eternal, that they [that is, we] might know thee the only true God, and Jesus Christ, whom thou has sent" (John 17:3). I stress that phrase, "the only true God."

One of the tragedies of our day is that the true God is not known. Tragically, contemporary Christianity has inherited the view of a capricious, imperious, and especially angry God whose primary duty is to frighten little children and add suffering to the lives of already staggering adults. May I unequivocally and unilaterally cry out against that sacrilegious and demeaning view of a loving and compassionate Father in Heaven. I wonder if the Savior may not have known, even in His mortal years, that this would happen, thus His plea for the world to know the true God, the fatherly God, the forgiving and redeeming and benevolent God. To bring that understanding was one of the reasons Christ came to the earth.

So feeding the hungry, healing the sick, rebuking cruelty, pleading for faith—and hope and charity—this was Christ showing us the way of the Father, He who is "merciful and gracious, slow to anger, long-suffering and full of goodness" (*Lectures on Faith* [1985], 42). In His life and especially in His death, Christ was declaring, "This is God's compassion I am showing you, as well as my own." It is the perfect Son's manifestation of the perfect Father's care. In Their mutual suffering and shared sorrow for the sins and heartaches of the rest of us, we see ultimate meaning in the declaration: "For God so loved the world, that he gave his only begotten Son, that whosoever believeth in him should not perish, but have everlasting life. For God sent not his Son into the world to condemn the world; but that the world through him might be saved" (John 3:16–17).

I bear personal witness of a living, loving God, who knows our names, hears and answers prayers, and cherishes us eternally as His children. I testify that there is no spiteful or malicious motive in Him. I testify that all He does (He who never sleeps nor slumbers) is seek for ways to bless us, to help us, and to save us. I pray that you will believe that and embrace it. I pray that you will strive to see the wonder and majesty of heaven's concern and compassion for us.

I testify that Joseph Smith's vision of the Father and the Son began a chain of events that would change—and save—the world if the world would but accept the divine beings that he saw. In the spirit of this testimony, may I conclude with a blessing upon you as you press forward in your most important work of being a mother. I bless you in "such a time as this" that you will grow more grateful, more peaceful, more certain of God's love, and more secure in your standing before Him than ever before. I bless you that with His unfailing companionship you will find your way through your most difficult days and receive answers to your earnest prayers.

I especially bless you if you are troubled about someone else—about your spouse, or your children, or your parents, or your friends. I bless you to know that God loves and honors the earnest pleadings you make and that He is pleased to rush to your aid, to assist in the problem at hand, and to heal not only your heart but the hearts of those about whom you worry and for whom you pray and sometimes weep.

I bless you to know that there are good days ahead, always, that the darkest clouds always part and the most fearful days always flee before the beneficent face of the Father, the redeeming grace of the Son, and the sweet influence of the Holy Ghost in our lives. In our time and in such a gospel as heaven has bestowed upon us, we have every reason to be happy and every cause to be filled with divine anticipation. May you trust forever in the God who gave you life and in His Beloved Son, whose Church this is and who paid the ultimate price to redeem your life and restore your soul.

Within the Clasp of Your Arms

JEFFREY R. HOLLAND

When Christ came to His final days with His disciples, He summarized all that He had said to them in one great reminder, fearing perhaps that when their own disappointments came or when pressures would increase, they might not be able to recall every commandment on every scroll and every teaching from every discourse. He then said, as if there were but one way to remember it all:

"A new commandment I give unto you, That ye love one another; as I have loved you, that ye also love one another.

"By this shall all men know that ye are my disciples, if ye have love one to another" (John 13:34–35).

The expression of that love, so characteristic of mothers, is the ultimate test of our loyalty to Him. It is our highest form of discipline.

All of us have seen this special miracle work again and again, whether that be in our own lives, in the lives of our families, or in the lives of those with whom we've shared some experience. I know many mothers who have been grateful for the help and love of others when their own efforts seemed not to yield fruit, despite the depth of their love.

I remember vividly, for example, the dreadful circumstance into which one young lady had managed to fall several years ago. She was a Latter-day Saint, and yet her very life seemed to be disintegrating before our eyes. As a result of trying to play with the net down, trying to live without rules and without restraint, she was experiencing the moral and spiritual stupefaction of a broken marriage, illicit moral behavior, dark drug abuse, and finally physical violence. She was descending into a personal hell from which no one seemed to be able to retrieve her and from which she personally did not have the wish or the will to turn away.

Her mother and others who had great concern for her had been in contact with me. Her Church leaders had tried to help. All seemed to no avail. The weeks became months, and human life unraveled before our eyes.

Then something happened. A lifelong friend of this young woman contacted her and tried, with love, to open her eyes and touch her heart. When neither her eyes nor her heart seemed to be yielding, this friend, this sister in the family of God who understood Paul's reminder that when one member suffers all suffer with it, grabbed the lapels of her friend's heavy winter coat and shook it with all her might. She shook her with all the strength her 105 pounds could muster, and, sobbing, she said through her tears, "Look at yourself. Don't you see what you are becoming? Look at yourself! I can't stand it anymore. I love you, and you are breaking my heart." At that she let go of the lapels of the big heavy coat and with tears streaming from her eyes turned and ran away.

The young lady whose life was in such jeopardy later recalled for me her response to that encounter. She said, "I don't know exactly what happened in that moment. Perhaps I am not likely ever to know. I had been talked to by many people, and little of it had meant anything to me. But if I live to be a hundred, I will never forget what I saw with my eyes and heard with my ears as this my childhood friend looked at me with utter anguish and screamed into my soul, 'I love you, and you are breaking my heart.'"

Today that girl is the beautiful, happy, safe, and productive young woman which she once had been and which surely God meant her to be. She has been remarkably successful in a graduate program at a very good university. She is fully active in the Church, and she is devoted to a life of responsibility and respectability—all because someone in her own way said at the right time and with the right intent that whatever disappointments there had been, these two were forever sisters and disciples of Christ. That stunning declaration not only changed a life, but it quite literally saved this one. We need such brothers and sisters nearby us.

In a world which has some strife and stress and disappointment, we will never have too much friendship or too many arms extended to bear us up and lead us forward. Of greatest importance, however, is the support we offer, the strength we gain, from each other within the embrace of our loving families.

A recent study conducted by the Church has forcefully confirmed statistically what we have been told again and again. That is, if loving, inspired instruction and example are not provided at home, then our related efforts for success in and around Church programs are severely limited. It is increasingly clear that we must teach the gospel to our families personally, live those teachings in our homes, or run the risk of discovering too late that a Primary teacher or priesthood adviser or seminary instructor *could* not do for our children what we *would* not do for them.

May I offer just this much encouragement regarding such a great responsibility? What I cherished in my relationship with my son Matt as he was growing up was that he was, along with his mother and sister and brother, my closest, dearest friend. I loved to be with him—and I still do. We talk a lot. We laugh a lot. We discuss problems. We compare notes and offer suggestions and share each other's challenges. I pray for him and have cried with him, and I'm immensely proud of him.

I felt I could talk to Matt throughout his teen years about how he was enjoying seminary because I tried to talk to him about all of his classes at school. We often imagined together what his mission would be like because he knew how much my mission meant to me. And he asked me about temple marriage because he knew I was absolutely crazy about his mother, and he wanted his future wife to be like her and for them to have what we have.

Now, I know that there are fathers and sons (and mothers and daughters) who feel they do not have any portion of what is here described. I know there are parents who would give virtually their very lives to be close again to a struggling child. I know there are children who wish their parents were at their side. I simply say to us all, young and old, never give up. Keep trying, keep reaching, keep talking, keep praying—but never give up. Above all, never pull away from each other.

I know so many mothers who berate themselves for their mistakes, for missed opportunities, for things said in the heat of the moment that they wish they could withdraw. You are not alone! May I share a brief but painful moment from my own efforts as a father.

Early in our married life my young family and I were laboring through graduate school at a university in New England. Pat was the Relief Society president in our ward, and I was serving in our stake presidency. I was going to school full-time and teaching half-time. We had two small children then, with little money and lots of pressures.

One evening I came home from long hours at school, feeling the proverbial weight of the world on my shoulders. Everything seemed to be especially demanding and discouraging and dark. I wondered if the dawn would ever come. Then, as I walked into our small student apartment, there was an unusual silence in the room.

"What's the trouble?" I asked.

"Matthew has something he wants to tell you," Pat said.

"Matt, what do you have to tell me?" He was quietly playing with his toys in the corner of the room, trying very hard not to hear me. "Matt," I said a little louder, "do you have something to tell me?"

He stopped playing, but for a moment he didn't look up. Then two enormous, tear-filled brown eyes turned toward me, and with the pain only a five-year-old can know, he said, "I didn't mind Mommy tonight, and I spoke back to her." With that he burst into tears, and his entire body shook with grief. A childish indiscretion had been noted, a painful confession had been offered, the growth of a five-year-old was continuing, and loving reconciliation could have been wonderfully under way.

Everything might have been just terrific—except for me. If you can imagine such an idiotic thing, I lost my temper. It wasn't that I lost it with Matt—it was with a hundred and one other things on my mind. But he didn't know that, and I wasn't disciplined enough to admit it. He got the whole load of bricks.

I told him how disappointed I was and how

84

much more I thought I could have expected from him. I sounded like the parental pygmy I was. Then I did what I had never done before in his life: I told him that he was to go straight to bed and that I would not be in to say his prayers with him or to tell him a bedtime story. Muffling his sobs, he obediently went to his bedside, where he knelt—alone—to say his prayers. Then he stained his little pillow with tears his father should have been wiping away.

If you think the silence upon my arrival was heavy, you should have felt it now. Pat did not say a word. She didn't have to. I felt terrible!

Later, as we knelt by our own bed, my feeble prayer for blessings upon my family fell back on my ears with a horrible, hollow ring. I wanted to get up off my knees right then and go to Matt and ask his forgiveness, but he was long since peacefully asleep.

My own relief was not so soon coming, but finally I fell asleep and began to dream, which I seldom do. I dreamed Matt and I were packing two cars for a move. For some reason his mother and baby sister were not present. As we finished I turned to him and said, "Okay, Matt, you drive one car and I'll drive the other."

This five-year-old very obediently crawled up on the seat and tried to grasp the massive steering wheel. I walked over to the other car and started the motor. As I began to pull away, I looked to see how my son was doing. He was trying—oh, how he was trying. He tried to reach the pedals, but he couldn't. He was also turning knobs and pushing buttons, trying to start the motor. He could scarcely be seen over the dashboard, but there staring out at me again were those same immense, tear-filled, beautiful brown eyes. As I pulled away, he cried out, "Daddy, don't leave me. I don't know how to do it. I'm too little." And I drove away.

A short time later, driving down that desert road in my dream, I suddenly realized in one stark, horrifying moment what I had done. I slammed my car to a stop, threw open the door, and started to run as fast as I could. I left car, keys, belongings, and all—and I ran. The pavement was so hot it burned my feet, and tears blinded my straining effort to see this child somewhere on the horizon. I kept running, praying, pleading to be forgiven and to find my boy safe and secure.

As I rounded a curve, nearly ready to drop from physical and emotional exhaustion, I saw the unfamiliar car I had left Matt to drive. It was pulled carefully off to the side of the road, and he was laughing and playing nearby. An older man was with him, playing and responding to his games. Matt saw me and cried out something like, "Hi, Dad. We're having fun." Obviously he had already forgiven and forgotten my terrible transgression against him.

But I dreaded the older man's gaze, which followed my every move. I tried to say "Thank you," but his eyes were filled with sorrow and disappointment. I muttered an awkward apology, and the stranger said simply, "You should not have left him alone to do this difficult thing. It would not have been asked of you."

With that, the dream ended, and I shot upright in bed. My pillow was stained, whether with perspiration or tears I do not know. I threw off the covers and ran to the little metal camp cot that was my son's bed. There on my knees and through my tears I cradled him in my arms and spoke to him while he slept. I told him that every dad makes mistakes but that they don't mean to. I told him it wasn't his fault I had had a bad day. I told him that when boys are five or fifteen, dads sometimes forget and think they are fifty. I told him that I wanted him to be a small boy for a long, long time, because all too soon he would grow up and be a man and wouldn't be playing on the floor with his toys when I came home. I told him that I loved him and his mother and his sister more than anything in the world, and that whatever challenges we had in life, we would face them together. I told him that never again would I withhold my affection or my forgiveness from him, and never, I prayed, would he withhold them from me. I told him I was honored to be his father and that I would try with all my heart to be worthy of such a great responsibility.

Well, you may feel that you are not a perfect mother. I know I have not proven to be the perfect father I vowed to be that night and a thousand nights before and since. But I still want to be, and I believe this wise counsel from President Joseph F. Smith: "If you will keep your [children] close to your heart, within the clasp of your arms; if you will make them to feel that you love them, . . . and keep them near to you, they will not go very far from you, and they will not commit any very great sin. But it is when you turn them out of the home, turn them out of your affection . . . that [is what] drives them from you. . . .

"If you wish your children to be taught in the principles of the gospel, if you wish them to love the truth and understand it, if you wish them to be obedient to and united with you, love them and prove to them that you do love them by your every word and act to[ward] them" (*Gospel Doctrine,* 5th ed. [1966], 282, 316).

We all know parenthood is not an easy assignment, but it ranks among the most imperative assignments ever given, in time or eternity. We must not pull away from our children. We must keep trying, keep reaching, keep praying, keep listening. We must keep them "within the clasp of [our] arms." That is what mothers and fathers are for.